JESUS AND THE CHILDREN
MATTHEW, 19:13-15

One day, some people brought their children to Jesus to bless them. Some disciples thought Jesus was too busy, but Jesus said, "Let the children come to me." He hugged them, put His hands on them, and blessed them, showing His love for all children.

THE PARABLE OF THE GOOD SAMARITAN
LUKE, 10:25-37

Jesus told a story about a man who was hurt and left on the road. Many people passed by him, but didn't help. Then, a Samaritan man, who was different from those who passed by, stopped. He took care of the man's wounds and brought him to a safe place to rest. Jesus said that we should love and help everyone, like the Good Samaritan did.

THE PARABLE OF THE PRODIGAL SON
LUKE, 15:11-32

Jesus told the story of a young man who spent all his money and was left alone. He was very sad and sorry. When he decided to go back home, his father saw him coming. Even after so many mistakes, his father welcomed him with a big hug and a party, happy to have him back. Jesus said we should forgive and love, just as the father loved his son.

JESUS'S TRIUMPHAL ENTRY INTO JERUSALEM
LUKE, 19:28-40

Jesus entered Jerusalem riding on a little donkey, and many people came to see Him. They spread their clothes and palm branches on the road and waved to Jesus, shouting, "Hosanna! Blessed is the one who comes in the name of the Lord!" Everyone was happy and honored Jesus, celebrating His arrival.

THE LAST SUPPER
MARK, 14:12-26

Jesus and his twelve disciples gathered for a special meal. During the meal, Jesus shared bread and wine with them and said that this was a way to remember Him.

He talked about love and unity. Jesus wanted them to always remember this night and the love they shared.

Jesus and the Garden of Gethsemane
Matthew, 26:36-46

Jesus went to a garden called Gethsemane to pray. He was sad and asked his friends to stay awake with Him. But they fell asleep. Jesus prayed to God, asking for strength. Even knowing that difficult times were coming, He trusted in God. When He returned, Jesus found His friends sleeping and woke them up.

THE RESURRECTION OF JESUS
MATTHEW, 28:1-10

After Jesus was placed in the tomb, Mary Magdalene and another Mary went to visit Him. When they arrived, a bright angel told them that Jesus had risen, just as He had promised! They saw the empty tomb and were very happy. Jesus appeared to them and said, "Do not be afraid, tell everyone that I am alive!"

JESUS APPEARS TO THE DISCIPLES
JOHN, 20:19-23

After resurrecting, Jesus did something wonderful. He appeared to His disciples, who were gathered in a room with the doors closed. They were surprised and happy to see Him! Jesus showed them His hands and His side to prove it was really Him. He said, "Peace be with you," and they felt great joy.

ASCENSION OF JESUS TO HEAVEN
ACTS, 1:6-11

Jesus took His disciples outside and said He would return to heaven, but would always be with them in their hearts. Then, a cloud took Him up, and He ascended to heaven. The disciples looked up, amazed. Two angels appeared and said that Jesus would come back one day. They were happy, knowing that Jesus would always love them.

THE HOLY SPIRIT ARRIVES AT PENTECOST
ACTS, 2:1-4

The disciples were gathered when something amazing happened. Suddenly, a strong wind filled the place, and tongues of fire appeared over each of them. It was the Holy Spirit arriving, just as Jesus had promised. The disciples began to speak in different languages and felt great joy and courage to tell everyone about Jesus.

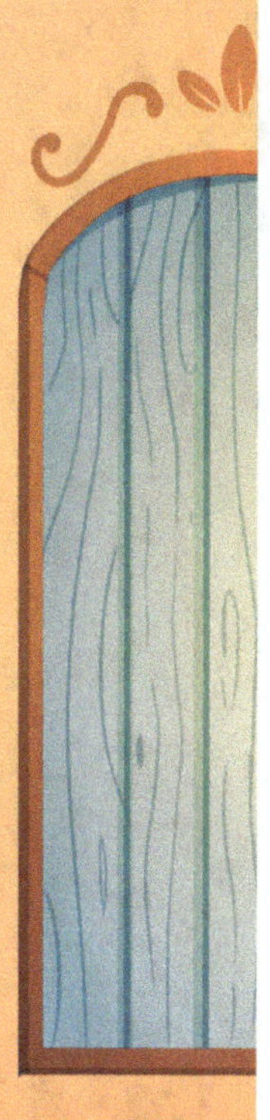